I0758667

BIG
Simple
Easy
To Colour

Toddler
Colouring Book
for Kids Ages 2-4

BELONGS TO:

....

by

Island Colors

If your child likes this coloring book
please leave a review.

Thank you -)

ISLAND COLORS

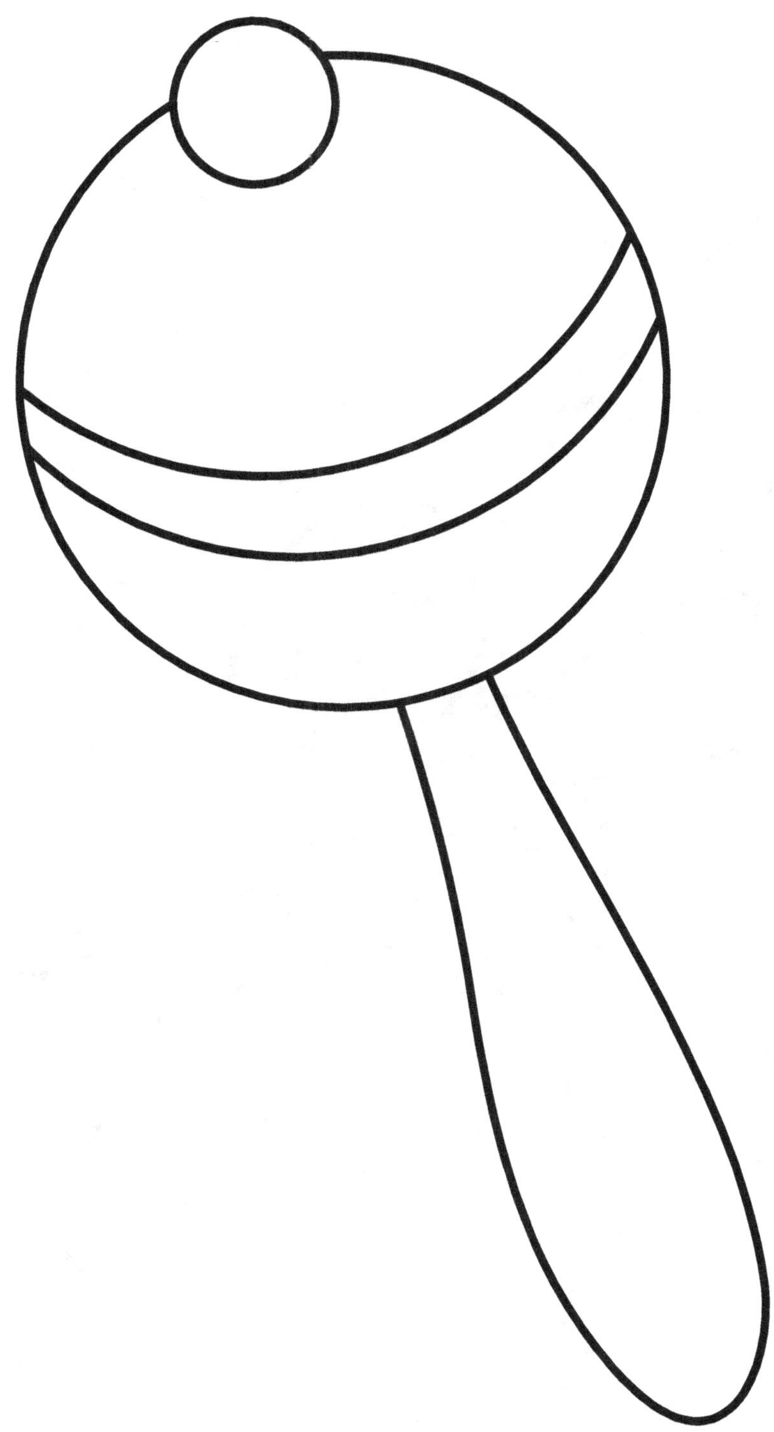

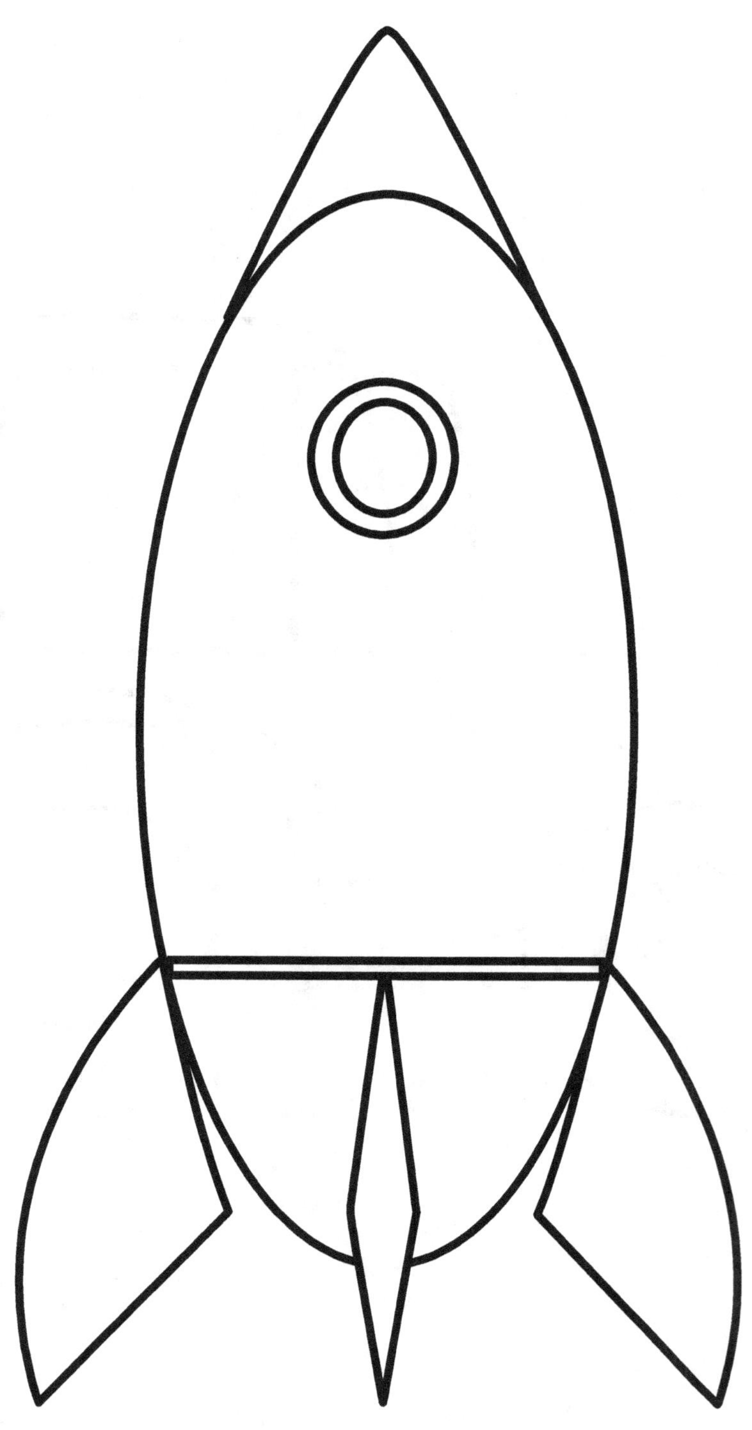

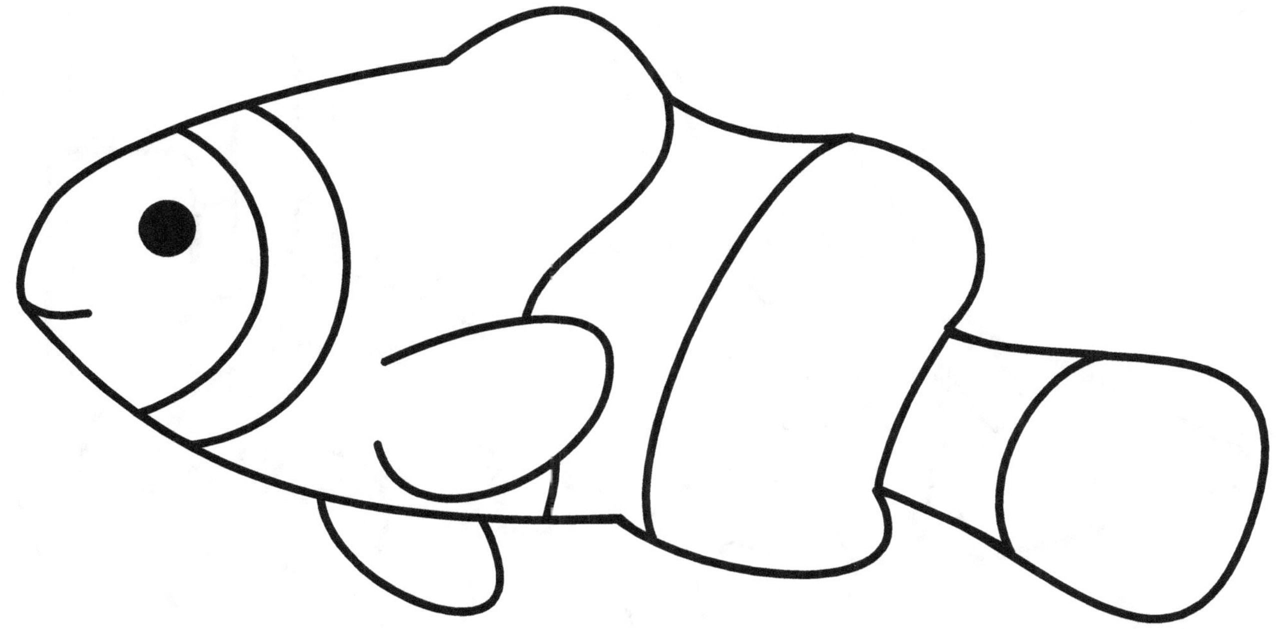

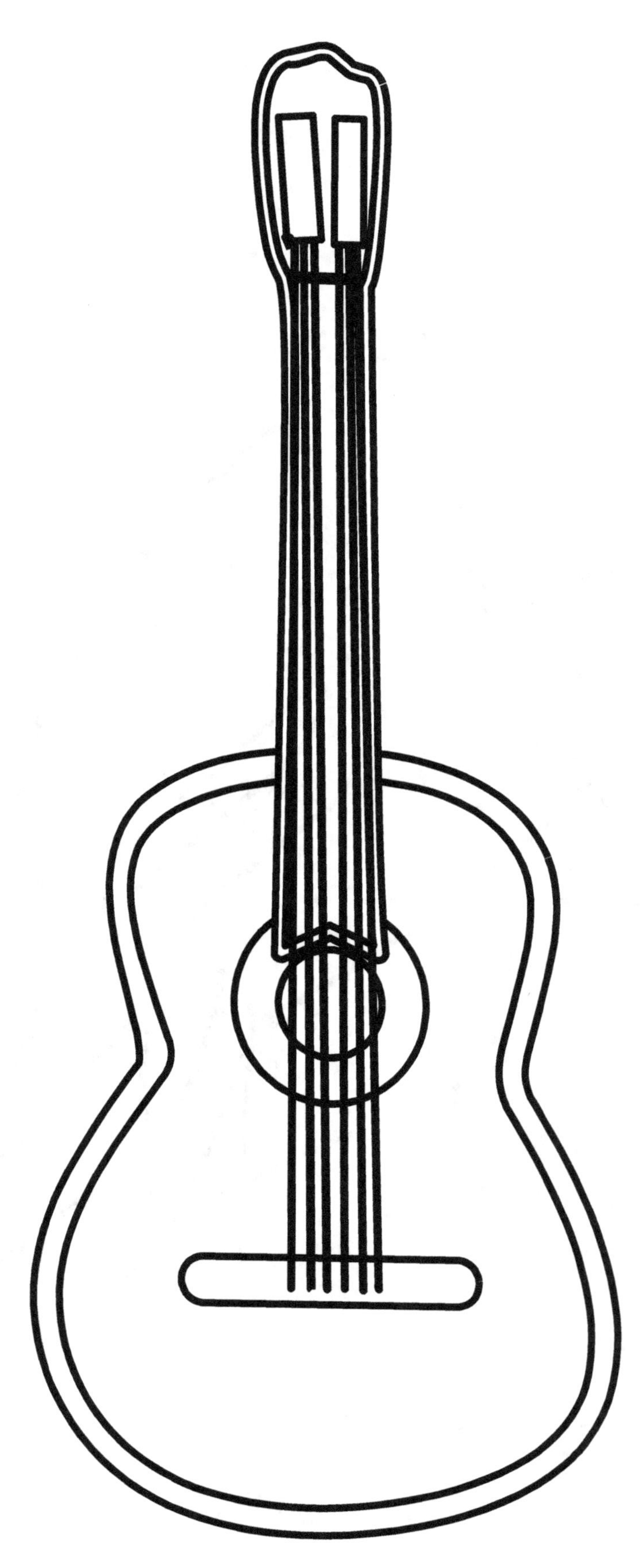

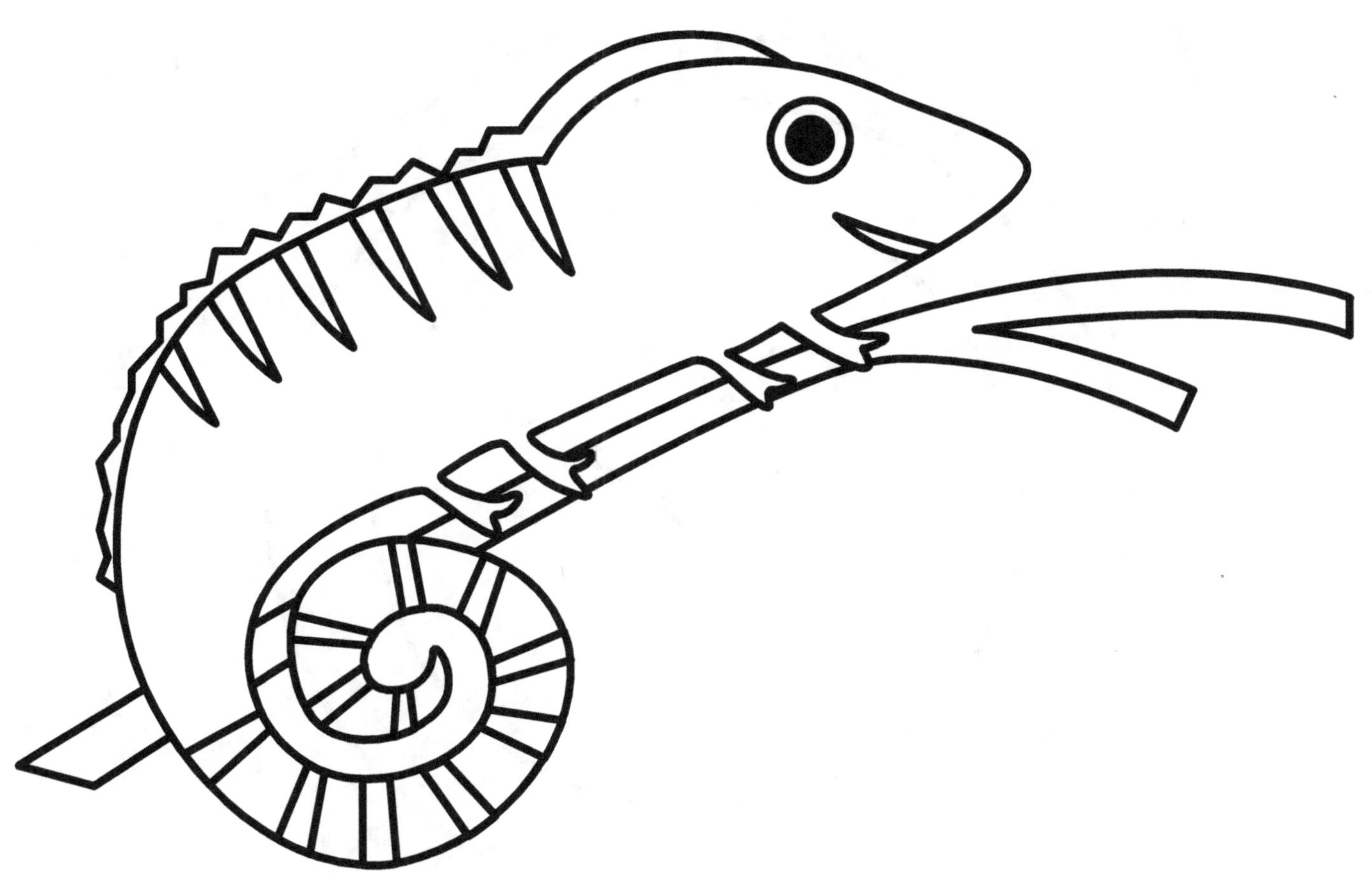

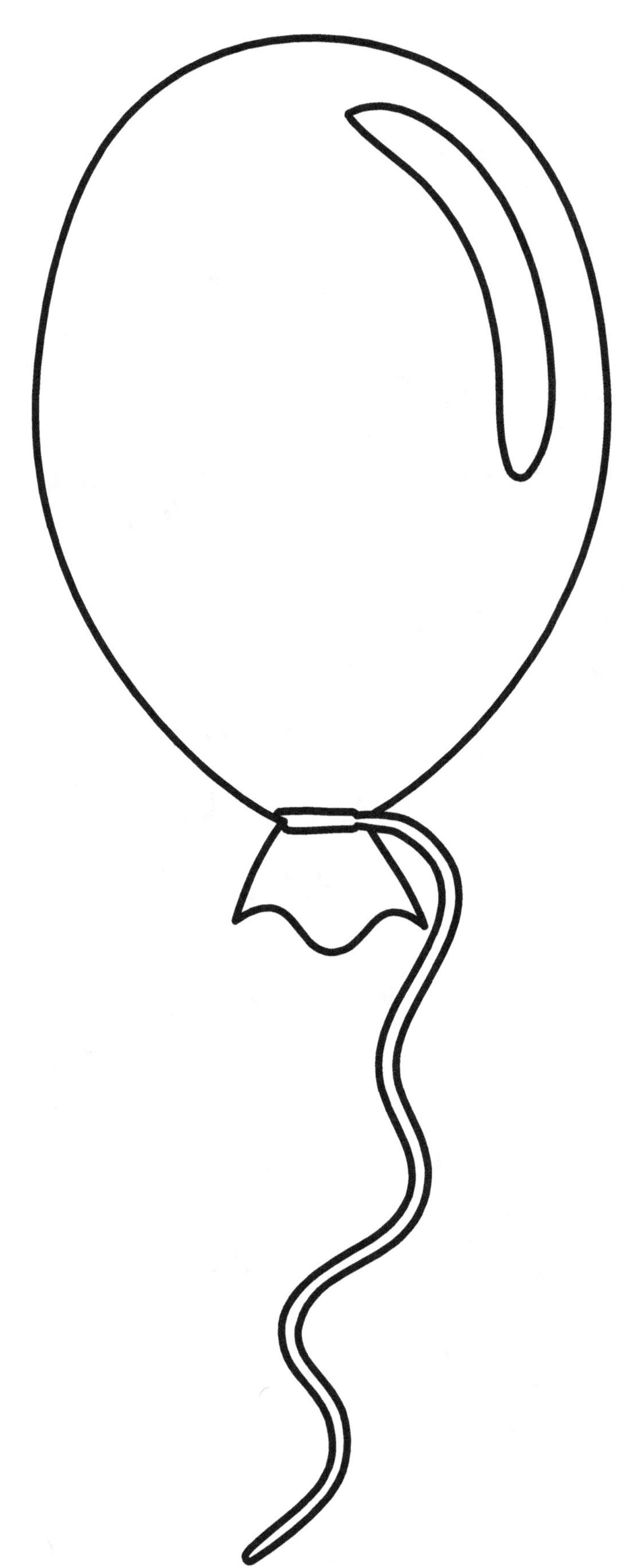

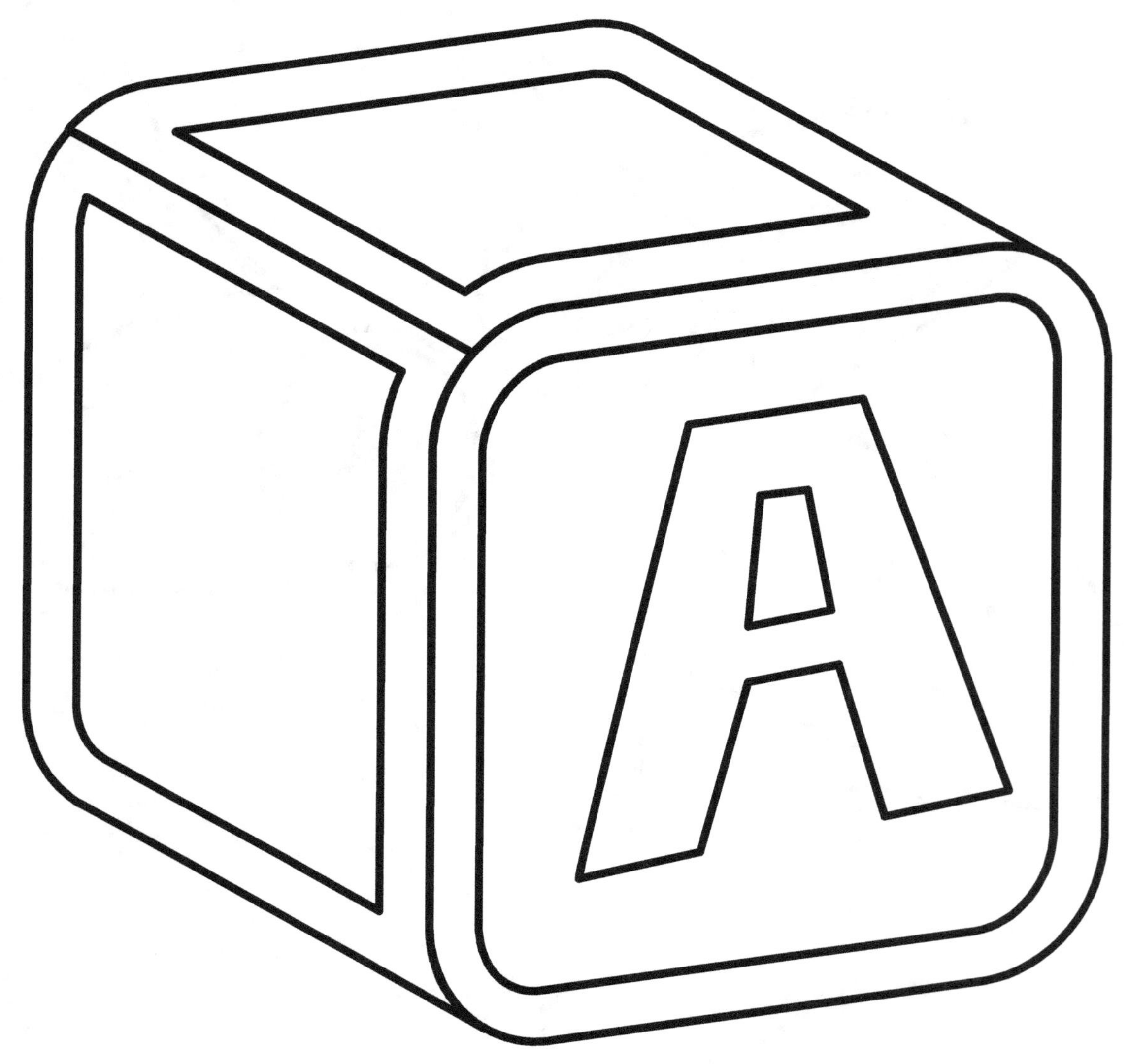

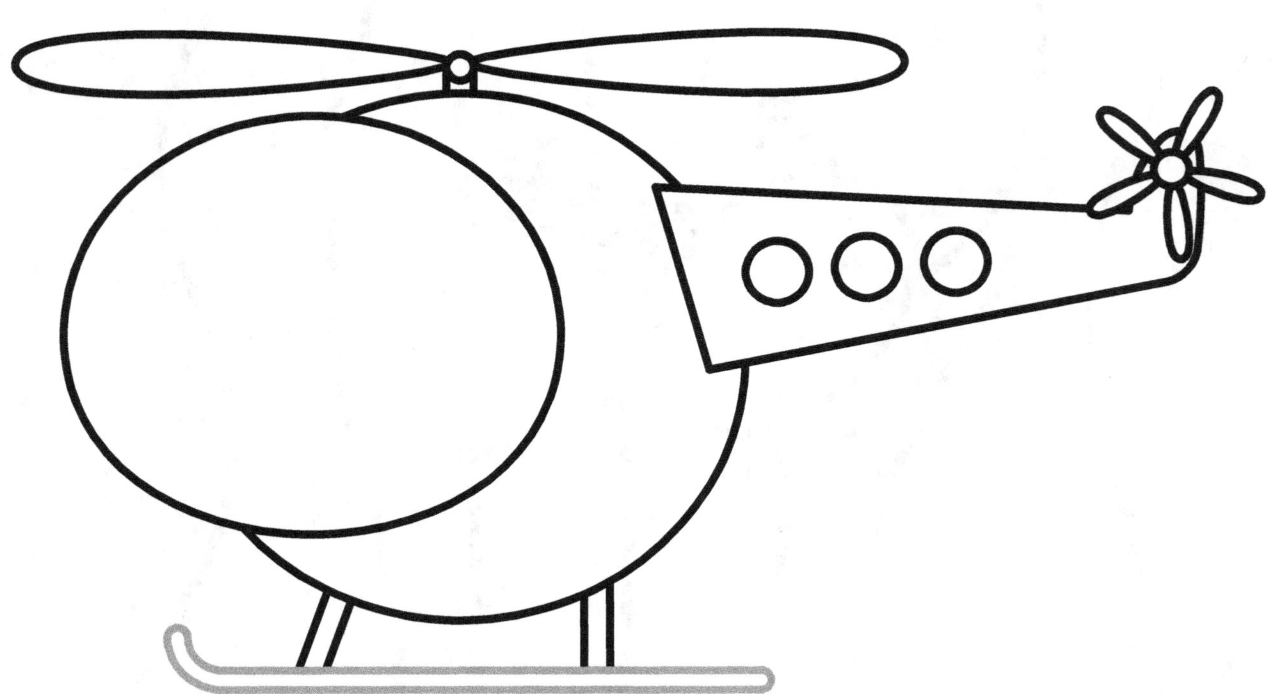

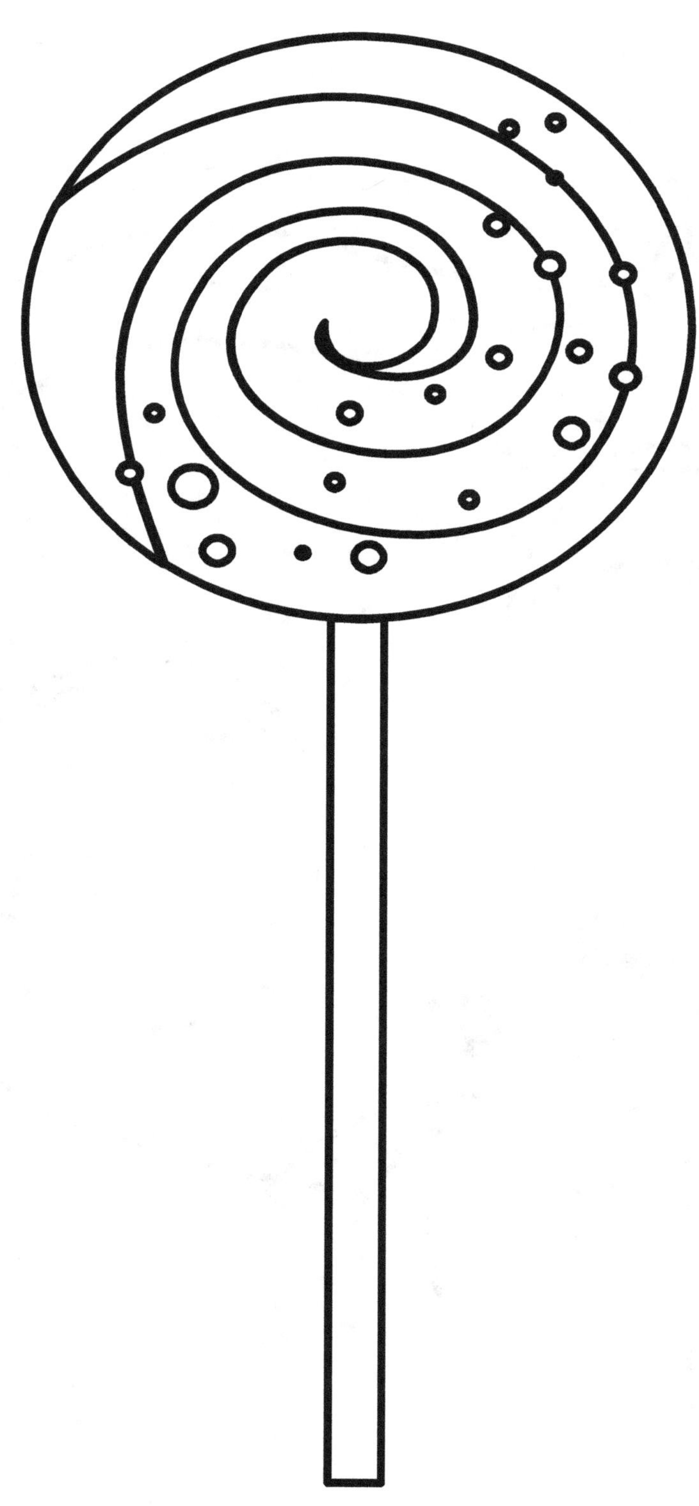

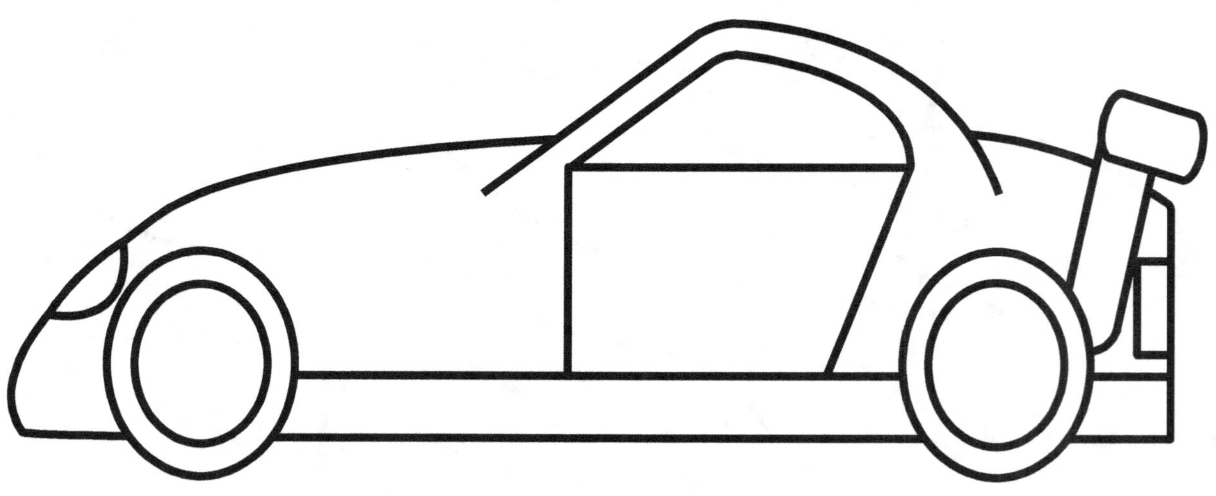

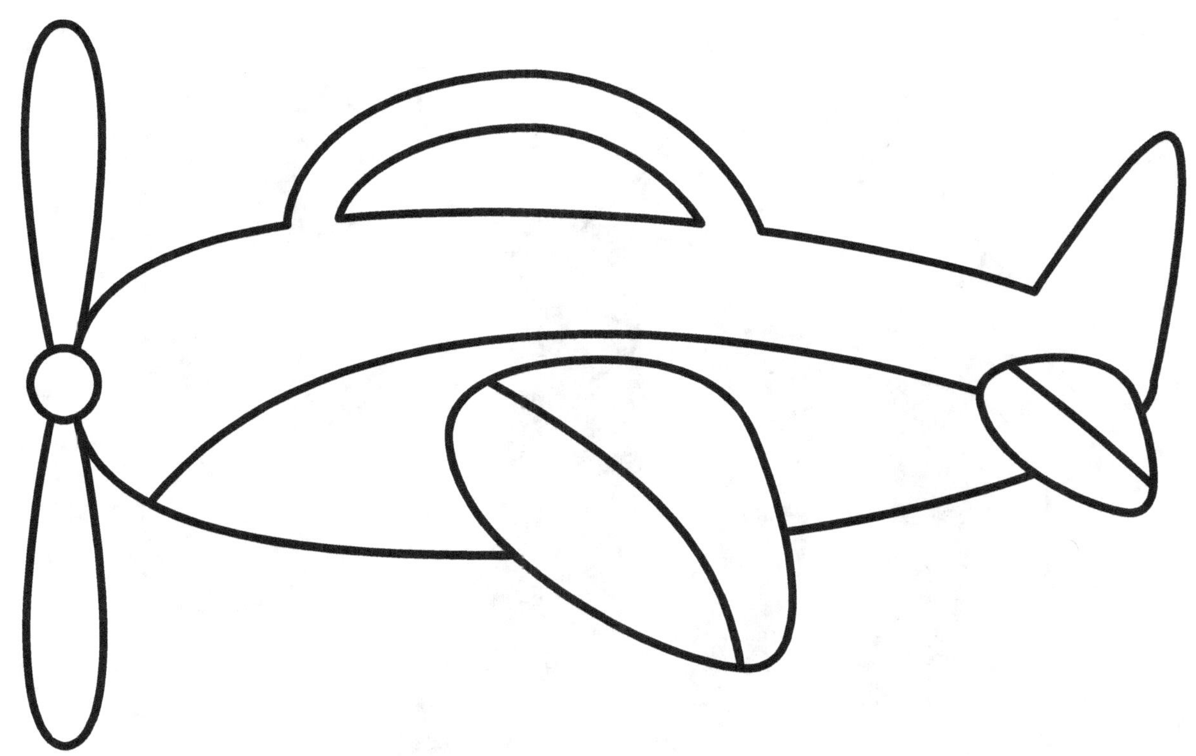

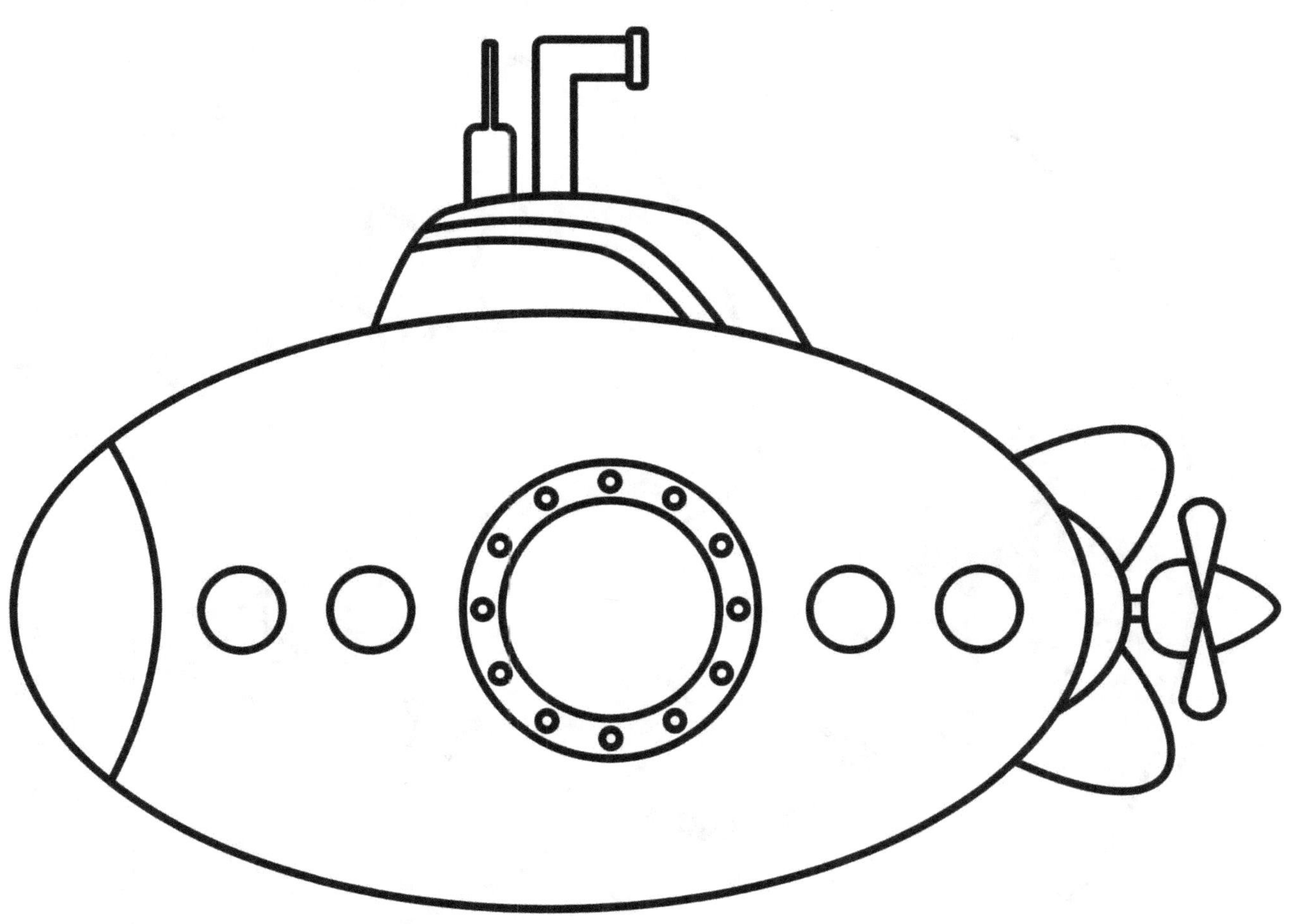

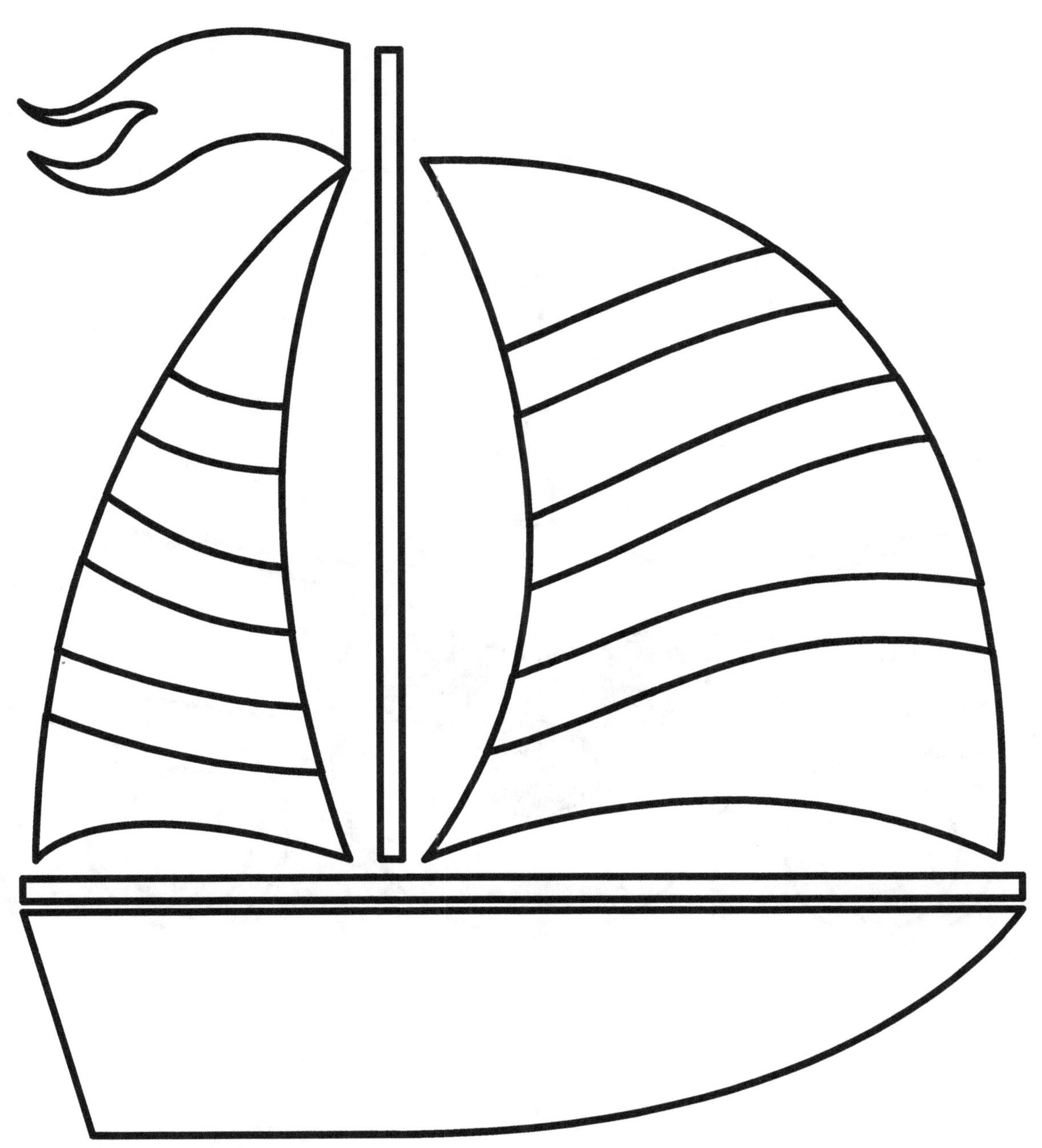

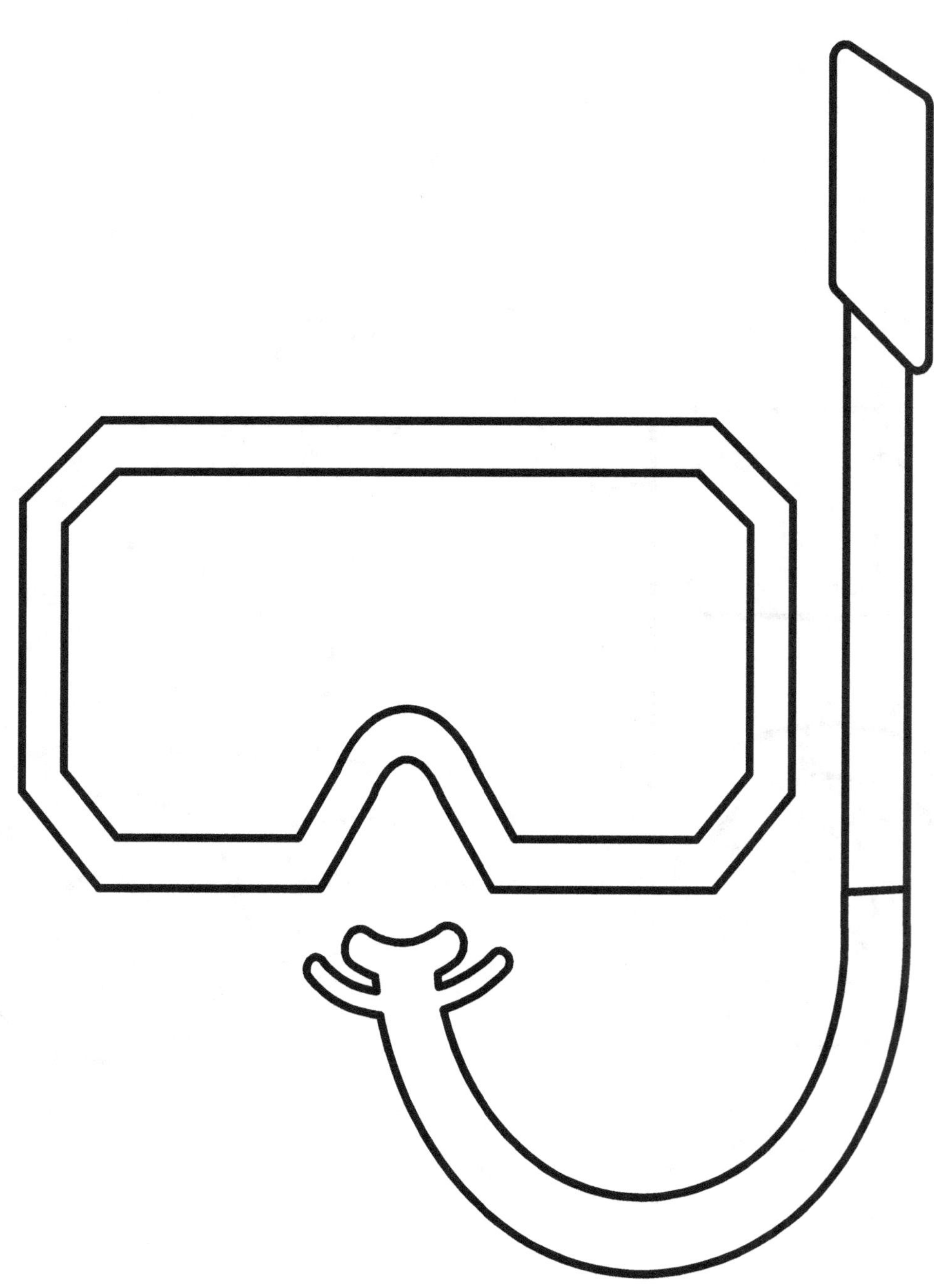

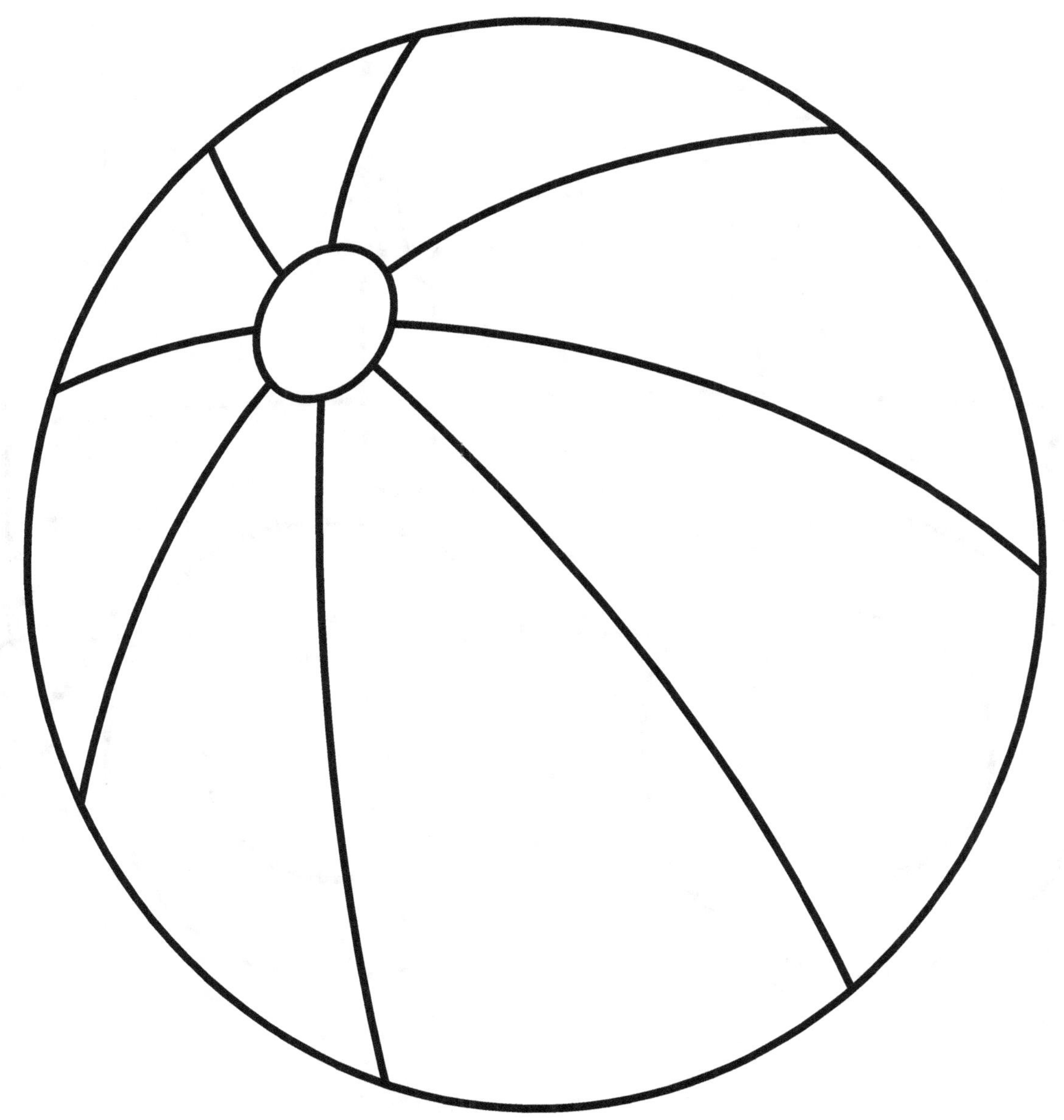

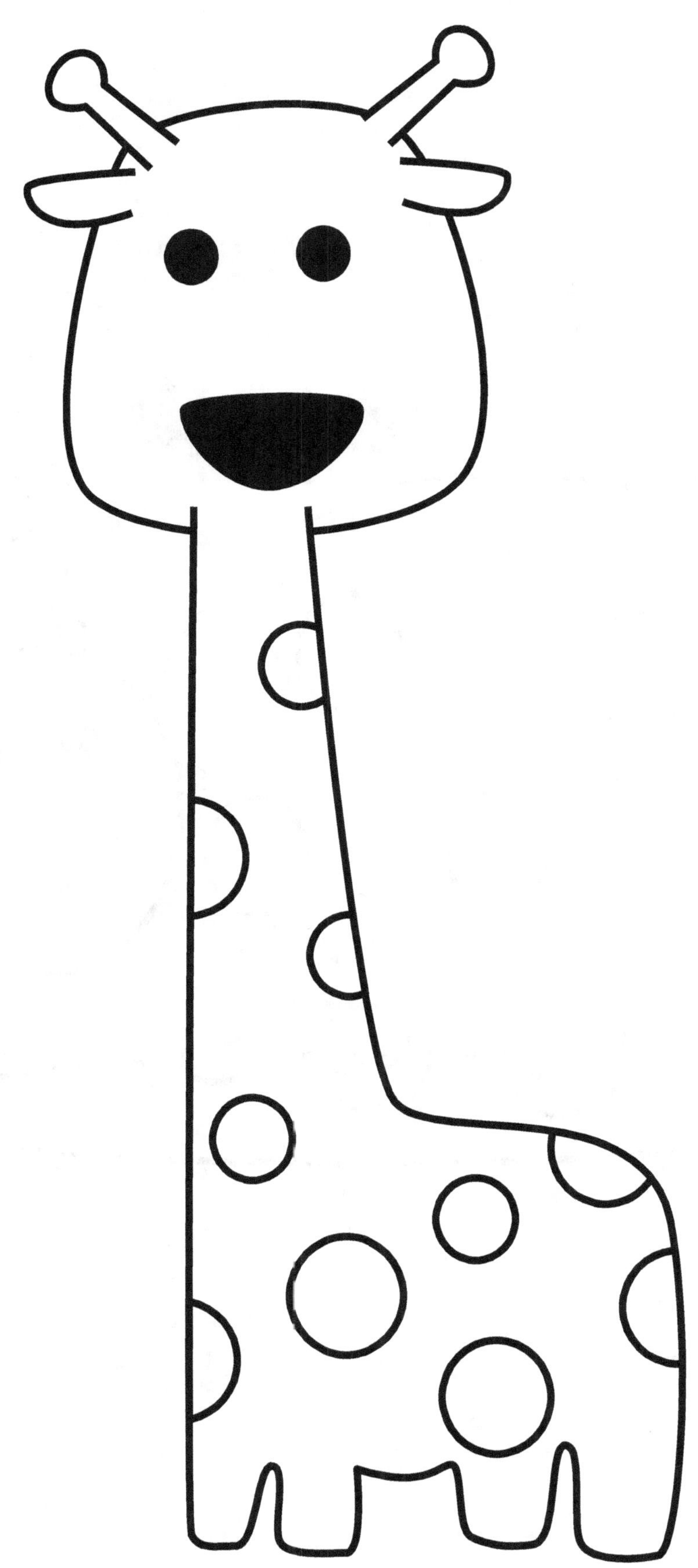

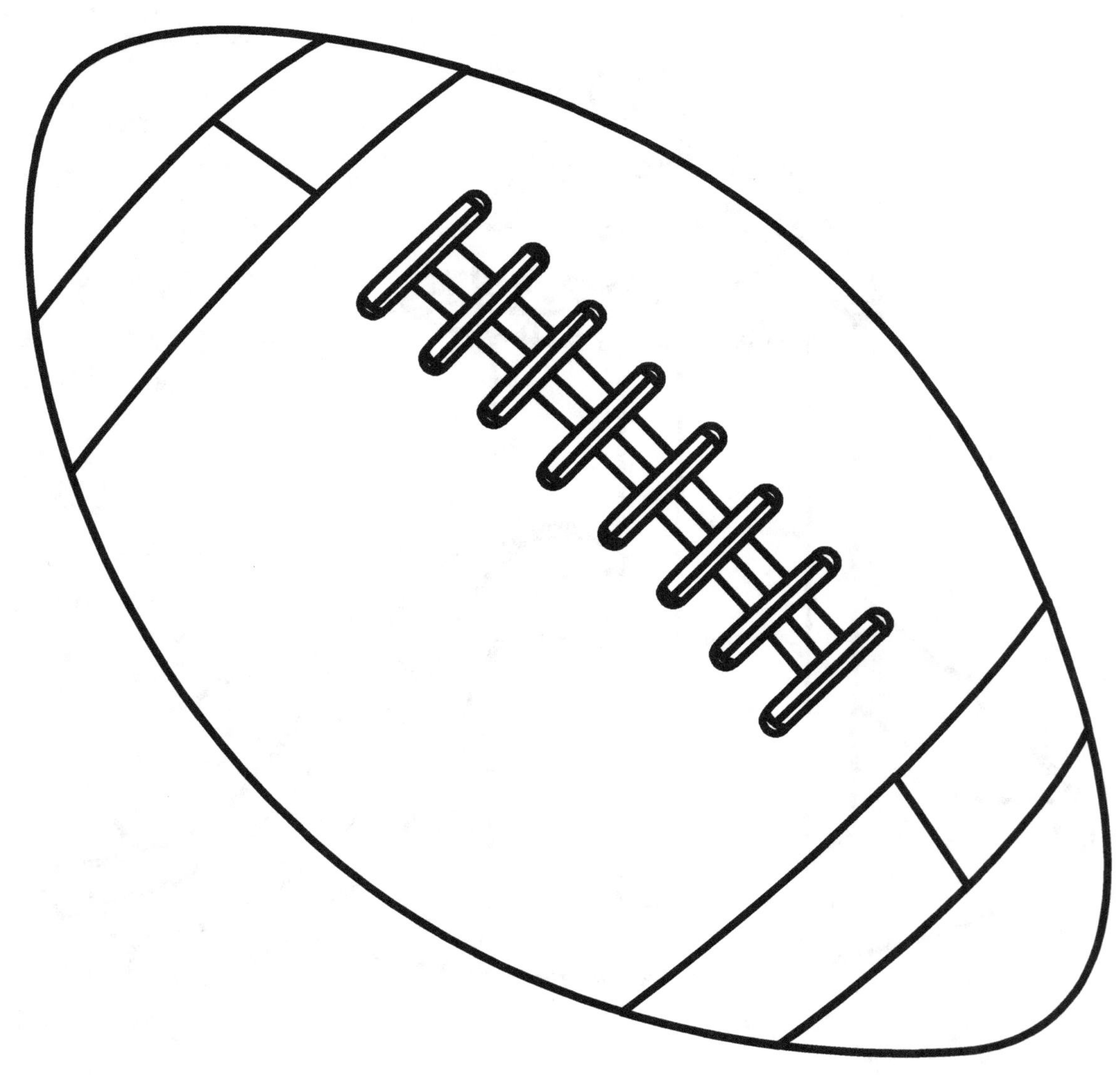

POLICE

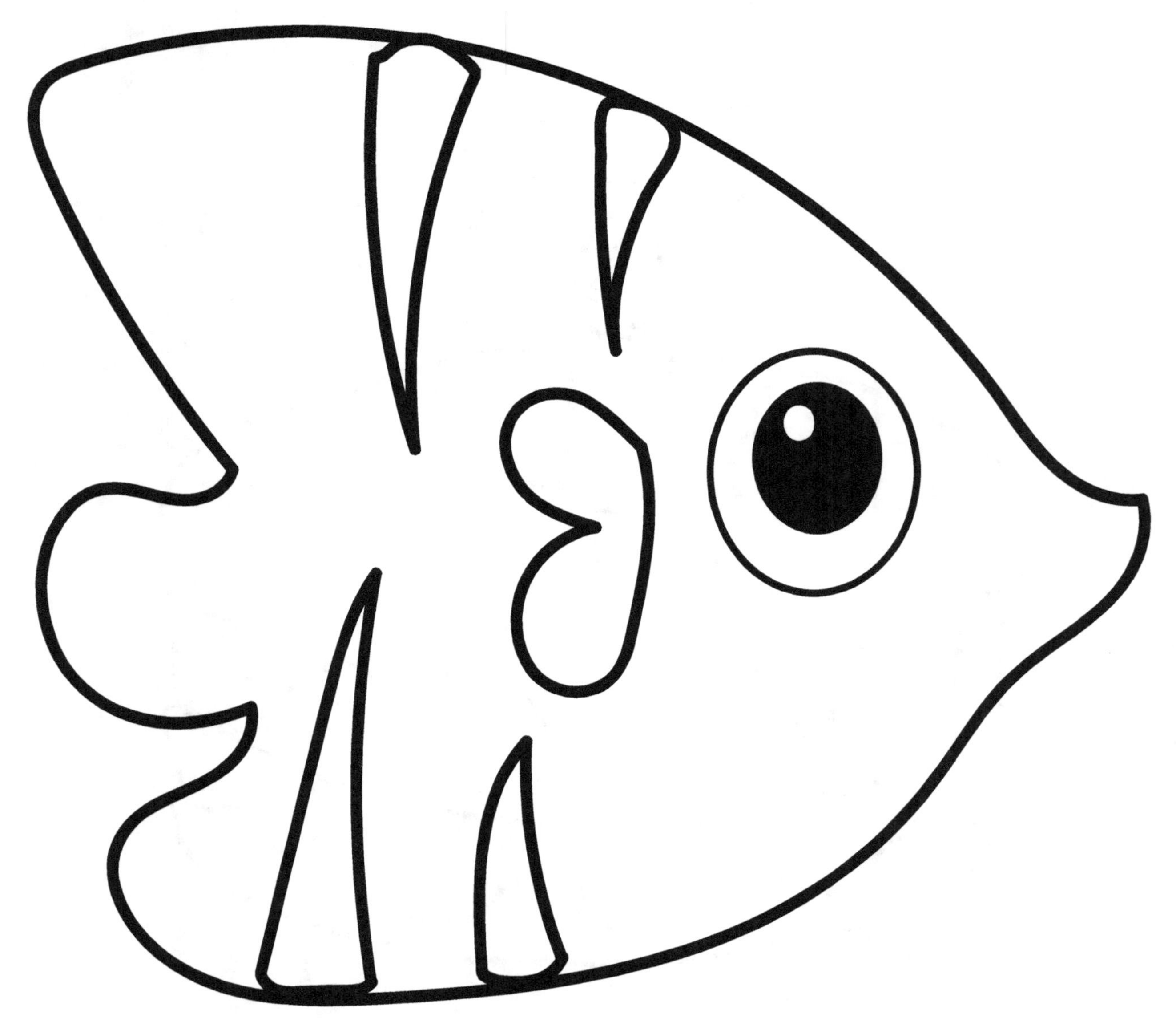

www.ingramcontent.com/pod-product-compliance
Lightning Source LLC
Chambersburg PA
CBHW080029260726
48658CB00007B/2538